NEW Z

FLORA AND FAUNA

Murdoch Riley

**Viking Sevenseas N.Z. Ltd; P.O. Box 152,
Paraparaumu, New Zealand**

Above: Toetoe Plumes (*Cortaderia* spp.) wave in the breeze.

As the proverb says: "The slightest movement of toetoe plumes can be seen, but not that of the heart" – *He tanga kākaho ka kitea e te kanohi; tēnā ko te tanga ngākau e kore e kitea.*

© Murdoch Riley
Revised Edition 2004
Viking Sevenseas N.Z. Ltd;
P.O. Box 152, Paraparaumu, New Zealand

ISBN 085467 110 2

Contents

Moss on Beech Stumps, Lake Sumner Forest Park (National Archives)

Flora   5

Vegetation – New Zealand trees – New Zealand –lilies – spiked, hooked and spiny plants – Parasites and epiphytes – Ferns – The rare and the beautiful

Fauna   32

New Zealand birds
New Zealand bats
New Zealand reptiles
New Zealand frogs
New Zealand snails
New Zealand insects

Great Spotted Kiwi at
Mt. Bruce Wildlife Centre,
Rod Morris Photographer,
Crown Copyright:
Dept. of Conservation,
Te Papa Atawhai 2004.

Flora

One tends to think of the vegetation of pre-European New Zealand as quietly evolving over many hundreds of thousands of years, being unaffected by land animals and without the presence of man to interfere with natural growth patterns. While it is true that higher forms of animal life were entirely absent and that man inhabited the country in a very sparse population distribution only in the last two thousand years, it is not correct to assume that the trees, flowers, shrubs, and other members of the plant family were not subject to harmful influences.

The popular belief of an isolated New Zealand developing as a lush Garden of Eden where primitive plant forms existed and other species evolved with quite unique characteristics is only partly true. In point of fact, New Zealand for the last million years or so, has been geologically unstable. Ice age followed ice age, gross climatic changes occurred, portions of land rose while other areas fell below sea level. With each advance of the ice sheet from South to North, as glaciers flowed further out from the bases of the mountain ranges, sub-tropical and temperate varieties of plants remained only in the northern parts of the country and in isolated pockets in the coastal lowlands.

During warm inter-glacial periods, plants tended to re-colonize previous habitats. However, many species did not survive the comparatively rapid climatic changes; some plants, in adapting to a new environment, changed the habit of the species so that almost unrecognizable new varieties developed. Although much work is still to be done in the field, the efforts of New Zealand plant palaeontologists

Tree ferns at Ball's Clearing Scenic Reserve, Puketitiri, Hawke Bay. Photograph by Deborah Shuker.

in dealing with the fossilized remnants of vegetable life, and particularly the micro-palaeontologists in their listing of pollens and other microscopic matter, have done much to establish the pattern of past changes.

It has become clear in recent years that in few other countries was the vegetative cover in such a flux of uncertainty as was the case in New Zealand in the last few hundred thousand years. The last major ice advance is dated at twelve to fifteen thousand years ago. The present inter-glacial period in which we live is subject to minor fluctuations with reason to believe that an upward temperature peak occurred around about one thousand years ago, well within the time of colonization by man.

The arrival of the original colonists at a time period of some two thousand years ago found them inhabiting a country in which vegetative cover was still evolving as a result of climatic and geological changes. Particularly is this so in the South Island where the flora was re-adjusting to an upward swing of temperature. On the other hand, much of the North Island was recovering from widespread ash showers created by incredible volcanic action which had recently changed the entire topography of the central North Island.

The early Māori were an agricultural people with a technology requiring them to burn and cultivate the land. Repeated use of fire as the mode of preparing farm land determined that by the time the earliest European botanists reached New Zealand, much forest area had been burnt off. Certainly this was the case where the density of the Māori people was high.

The coming of the European with the introduction of mammals, both domesticated and liberated for sport; the planting of large areas of grasslands with imported pasture species; and the land engineering works that have accompanied a sophisticated technology, have advanced the rate of change in both the flora and avifauna. These changes have been mainly to the disadvantages of the native species and, when this has been realised, steps have been taken to ensure that indigenous elements have not been entirely lost.

As the result of enlightened policies of forest preservation, wholly protected national parks and reserves have been established on a scale that are a tribute to the determination of both Māori and white immigrant to ensure retention of the character of at least a part of this country in its primitive form. These parks and reserves are for the use of the public and occupy no less than one fifth of the forests and mountain land.

Visitors to New Zealand are invariably impressed by the greenness of the country and the remarkable variation of scenery within a restricted area. In truth, the varied character of the vegetation to which the country owes its characteristic greenness is in fine harmony with the multi-formity of the geographical features.

A study of the botanical elements in New Zealand flora leads many authorities to support the belief that at various periods in its distant past the country was joined by land bridges extending into the south-eastern Pacific, now represented by isolated islands, the Solomon Islands Group, through the Malaysian Archipelago to mainland Asia. Similar studies have advanced the hypotheses of other land bridges through the Antarctic Continent to South America, Australia and South Africa, cumulatively called Gondwanaland. There is certainly much evidence of the many similarities between the botany of these areas and that of New Zealand, and so the plant scientist adds his evidence to that of other scientific disciplines.

Whatever the original source of the indigenous flora, there is no question that the plant life which developed in New Zealand was in many respects very different from that found elsewhere.

The northern forests of New Zealand are composed largely of plants derived from tropical ancestry. The forests of the south show distinct traces of sub-Antarctic origin. New Zealand forests are characterised by a profusion of climbers and epiphytes (a non-parasitic plant which is physically supported by another plant). Epiphytes and climbers of various sorts are usually associated with sub-tropical rain forests and are widespread throughout the country. Only a handful of trees are deciduous. An unusually high proportion of plants show distinctive juvenile and adult forms, sometimes so different as not to be recognisable as being the same variety. A surprising number of plants are unique in that they are the only known members of their family. These and other features of the indigenous flora that are described now add up to a complex enigma, which offers untold fascination fort the botanist and keen amateur observer.

KAURI (*Agathis australis*): See photo page 22. A tree of the family Araucariaceae from which also comes the South American "Monkey Puzzle" tree and the Norfolk Pine. The kauri is said to produce timber of better quality than that of any known pine. It has a beautiful and distinctive grain and a wonderful golden colour.

It is quite the most magnificent tree of the New Zealand forest, growing up to 60m. high and 11m. in girth, unbroken by any branch up to 30m. It was early recognised by Europeans as one of the most valuable timber trees of the world. Shortly after explorer Captain Cook returned to England from his first visit to New Zealand the British Navy despatched two ships to this country to load kauri for masts and spars. The timber was taken from Coromandel Peninsula in the north-eastern corner of the North Island and the peninsula was named for one of the ships, H.M.S. Coromandel.

The kauri tree has only been found north of latitude 38 degrees although in pre-historic times it had a wider distribution. Today only very limited stands remain, a tribute perhaps to its commercial value. The most accessible of the remaining kauri forests are found on the east coast of Northland. As with many New Zealand trees, kauri are slow growing, the largest taking up to 1,500 years to mature.

Kauri gum, an exudation from the kauri, was in itself a commercial product of some value, used in early colonial times as an important export for the making of linoleum, paints and varnishes. Kauri gum does not rot when buried in the ground and some gum found there points to the great antiquity of the species. The Māori used the gum as a mastigory. They also burnt the gum and used the soot obtained to sprinkle on the incised wounds made when tattooing a person. This gave permanency to the tattoo.

TŌTARA (*Podocarpus totara*): The tōtara is a tree growing up to 30m. in height. Its wood is red, straight-grained, very durable in the earth, resistant to attacks of toredo, or ship worm, short in the grain and thus liable to break under load without warning. It is hardy, slow-growing, and peculiar to New Zealand. Tōtara is found all over New Zealand from sea level to an altitude of 600m. A related species, Hall's tōtara, *P. hallii*, may be found above this elevation. The Māori preferred tōtara trunks to hollow out for their canoes because of their lightness, length and durability. Tradition acknowledges that tōtara was a direct descendant of Tāne, god of the forest, and Mumuwhango. In South Island legend it is one of the five trees in which the spark of fire is kept, and indeed it is inclined to spark and eject particles when burnt as firewood.

KAHIKATEA (*Podocarpus dacrydiodes*): See photo page 20. Sometimes known as the White Pine, this tree is New Zealand's tallest indigenous specimen, rising to 60m. The natural habitat of the kahikatea is in swamp land and the timber produced is very light in colour, practically without grain, very easily worked and sufficiently odourless to have been used in the past for butter and cheese boxes. A tradition of the Ngāti Pōtiki tribe links the kahikatea with their ancestor Pourangahua, who, it is said, came back to this country on the back of a giant bird. He had been living at Hawaiki, the Māori Eden, and persuaded the leading chief there to allow him to fly back on the bird to New Zealand. Nearing the end of his flight he plucked out some feathers from under the bird's wings and dropped them into the ocean. From the feathers a lofty plume-like tree rose out of the ocean, the kahikatea. A branch of the tree is said to have floated ashore to create the plantations of today's kahikatea.

HOROEKA (*Pseudopanax crassifolium*): Known as the Umbrella Tree, the Fishbone Tree, but more commonly as the Lancewood. Its young, unbranched form has very thick rigid sword-like leaves almost 1m. in length, sloping downwards from the stem. In its adult form at 15- 20 years of age it is a round-headed tree up to 15m. tall.

RIMU (*Dacrydium cupressinum*): The Red Pine. This has been an important timber tree until recent years when its scarcity has confined its use. Another unique indigenous tree that is also one of the country's oldest. Its pollen has been found in identical fossil form dating back 70 million years. The rimu grows in three distinct stages: the juvenile that is one of the most beautiful trees of the forest, with pale green weeping branches of very delicate appearance; the intermediate stage with its cone-like form common to the cypress of northern latitudes; and the adult (in appearance quite unlike the other two forms) that grows to 40 – 60m with a straight branchless trunk and a rounded top. Adult trees can be up to 1000 years old.

There are two hundred and more New Zealand plants that exhibit the phenomenon of the rimu in passing through two or more distinct changes in form during successive periods of growth. One can just imagine the difficulties in classification for the earliest European botanists. It has been suggested that rapid geological and climatic changes may have been contributing factors, but no one knows for sure, and a plant like rimu that has endured for 70 million years should surely be allowed to change its garb at will!

As with kauri gum, that of the rimu was burnt to make soot (called ngāpara) and used by the Māori in making tattooing pigment. Its gum was also used as an astringent in dressing severe wounds, as was its bark. Very long spears were fashioned from rimu wood. These were used before the introduction of firearms by defenders of a pā to thrust through the palisades at close quarters against the legs and bodies of the invaders.

MOUNTAIN BOG PINE (*Dacrydium bidwillii*): This is a shrub or small tree growing to 3.5m. in height in boggy ground or moor land. Again, there is a marked dissimilarity between the long narrow leaves of the juvenile tree and the scale-like leaves of the adult which lie close to the branches. During the transition stage the two leaf forms may be seen on the one tree.

Young Rimu Seedlings (National Archives)

Above: Tānekaha Trees, Harihari, South Westland (National Archives)
Below left: Strawberry Fungus (National Archives)
Below right: Mountain Beech Flowers, Tawhairauriki (National Archives)

TĀNEKAHA (*Phyllocladus trichomanoides*): Known as the Celery Pine because of the appearance of its leaf stalks which are so enlarged and flattened out as to appear to be true leaves somewhat resembling those of celery. The absence of leaves, with their normal function taken over by stems, is an adaptation of some plants in hot and arid regions. The anomaly with the tānekaha lies in that its normal habitat is below the canopy of a sub-tropical rain forest. Similar anomalies are seen in other New Zealand plants, with exaggerated differences appearing between two plants of the same species, where one is growing in direct sunlight and the other in the shade of the forest canopy. The tree grows to a height of around 20m.

Tānekaha has the meaning of "strong" or "virile" in the Māori language. Like the rimu tree it is the result of the union of Tāne, god of the forest, and Tūwaerore. Young saplings of the tree were used to make spring traps to catch birds, for fishing rods and for walking sticks. Its bark produces a reddish-brown dye used on ornamental parts of garments. In World War One the uniforms of N.Z. soldiers were dyed a khaki colour with tānekaha pigment.

TOATOA: MOUNTAIN CELERY PINE (*Phyllocladus aspleniflorus* var. *alpinus*): A close relative of the Celery Pine that also bears no true leaves but only flattened stems. It has, in addition, the curious growth characteristic of rooting from the ends of the lower branches which bend down to touch the ground. From this natural layering new trees arise and in their turn propagate in the same way. Thus does a parent tree form the centre of a series of rings moving further outwards with each succeeding generation.

PYGMY PINE (*Lepidothamnus laxifolius*): Reputed to be the smallest pine in the world. Fully matured trees of less than 7.5cm. in height can sometimes be found in fruit. Although so short in height, the flowers and fruit are the same size as its giant relation, the rimu, whose Māori name it also carries. In a favourable situation it will grow to a straggling shrub a metre high, while on very poor ground, for instance dry pumice soil, it forms a prostrate cushion plant.

KIEKIE (*Freycinetia baueriana*): A curious climbing shrub related to the Pandanus as found in tropical regions. The kiekie will grow across the forest floor until it reaches a suitable tree and will use a series of support roots to reach the upper levels of the forest. The leaves grow in spiral tufts along a rope-like stem 2cm. or more in thickness. The long fibrous leaves were used by the Māori in the manufacture of baskets, mats and belts, while the young bracts of fruit (tāwhara) were a source of food.

NĪKAU (*Rhopalostylis sapida*): The world's most southerly growing palm, and the only one native to this country. It can be found as far south as 44°. Of elegant and graceful appearance the nïkau grows in thick forests reaching a height as great as 10m. Purple panicles of waxy flowers grow strikingly at the base of the leaves and yield to equally attractive brilliantly scarlet berries. The leaves made an excellent thatch for houses of the Māori. Each leaf division is a small channel through which the water runs. A nïkau thatching will keep the interior of a building perfectly dry even when the construction is so open that sunlight penetrates the thatching. As well as shelter, food was provided to the Māori from the centre shoot, or rito; however, the act of taking the rito will kill the whole plant.

The Lily Family:

KAREAO (*Ripogonum scandens*): Its common name is Supplejack and it is a curious example of the family Liliacae. The long ropey lianes of this plant are a common sight in the forest, binding one tree to another, forming loops and twists and in the olden days making the forest virtually impassable. Many a horse and his rider came to grief in colonial times because of supplejacks. The black and brown stems often reach 13 to 20m. in length, the flowers are small, green and inconspicuous, formed at the end of the stems, the flowers yielding to brilliant scarlet berries. Kareao is said to have sprung from bits of the tail of Tunaroa, a water monster vanquished by Māui, the Polynesian man-god of legend.

The thin wiry stems of the supplejack are strong, tough and sufficiently flexible to be used as rope. The Māori found these stems of considerable use in the making of baskets, binding fences and rafts, building the framework of houses, and the manufacture of rope ladders to scale steep river and beach cliffs. A strange member of the lily family indeed.

TĪ KŌUKA (*Cordyline australis*): The "Cabbage Tree" (page 22) is yet another atypical example of a lily. One of the most striking features of the open plains of New Zealand, the cabbage tree lends a peculiarly tropical setting to the landscape. The common English name for the tree arises from the wasteful practice of early European settlers in using the young tender heads as a substitute for cabbage. Wasteful, since this kills the tree. Young trees are unbranched, the stem rising to a bushy head some 3 to 13m. high. After flowering the crown divides into two and an old tree can be many-branched. The leaves are long, sword-like and fibrous. These leaves, up to one metre in length, yield a fibre which was used by the Māori for making superior quality cordage. The small white flowers, showing distinct lily characteristics, grow in heavy panicles, perfuming the air for quite a distance around the flowering tree with a heavy sweet smell. The stem, or trunk, differs very much from the anatomy of true trees and while normally up to 1.5m. through, can on occasion grow very large indeed. Colenso, one of the early botanical explorers of New Zealand, reported that he had seen a cabbage tree with the trunk hollowed out to form a capacious storeroom. The tree exhibits a survival trait which is shared with a number of similar local plants in being almost immune to fire. After severe forest fires cabbage trees, nīkau palms and several varieties of tree ferns continue to grow and apparently thrive on the richly ash-covered ground, and from the absence of competition. In fact the cabbage tree exhibits an enormous vitality and tenacity for life. An example has been recorded of a number of sections of stems of cabbage trees being disposed of on a tidal mud flat where they lay, alternatively covered with salt water and exposed to the sun. After experiencing this treatment for eight months, a particularly high tide lifted them on to reasonably high ground where they rooted and grew. There are several other species of *Cordyline* endemic to New Zealand but they are small in habit and have a more limited distribution than *C. australis*.

HARAKEKE (*Phormium tenax*): See photo page 20. New Zealand Flax is native only to this country and Norfolk Island. It is not a true flax although its fibres have flax-like qualities. A swamp and hillside dweller, harakeke comes in many varieties, usually having dark green leaves that extend to 3m. in length rising from a central saddle. The flower stalks rise to 5m. in height and bear a profusion of dark red flowers which are pollinated by nectar eating birds.

The Māori prepared and used flax fibre in almost every aspect of their technology. Indeed, one leading chief in colonial days, in finding out that flax was not grown in England, asked how could one possibly manage without it. For a long time colonists found good use for flax fibre too, in making cordage for rope, for agricultural twine, for wool packs and floor coverings.

Māori plaited from flax a wide assortment of baskets, dishes for food, drinking cups, floor and sleeping mats. Flax threads were made into ropes for cliff ladders, fishing lines and nets, eel-pots, lines for kites and whipping tops. The leaves used in the making of poi balls, musical trumpets, toboggans, flat belts to support the injured on litters, head and waist bands, wristlets, anklets, sandals - the list is endless.

Cushion Plants:

A curious class of plants in which the normal growth is in low, compact masses, is sometimes referred to as cushion plants. This form is an adaptation to an extreme climate and many parts of the world have no native examples. Cushion plants are common in the South American Andes and are seen on other mountain ranges. New Zealand possesses examples, and what is quite exceptional, is that the natural habitat of some local varieties are in lowland regions as distinct from the mountainous habitat usual in other countries.

VEGETABLE SHEEP (*Raoulia* and *Haastia* spp.): Both of these genera contain cushion-like plants bearing the common name of Vegetable Sheep that look in the distance not unlike a flock of sheep. On shingle slides and dry banks the plants form large rounded or oddly shaped mounds of highly compacted growth. These mounds vary in size from 25cm. across to 2m. across, but seldom rise higher than 60cm. The branches divide again and again towards the tips which are covered with small woolly leaves packed very tightly together. Long velvety hairs overlap around each branch and over the leaves to quite hide the structure of the plant. Within this compacted outer mass of bifurcated branches, woolly leaves and hairs, rotting vegetation and branches form a peat-like mould which holds water and into which the branch tips root. The outward colour is cream to silvery, depending on whether the flowers are out or not.

GIANT VEGETABLE SHEEP (*Haastia pulvinaris*): While *H. pulvinaris* shares its "vegetable sheep" name with the *Raoulia* spp; it has an entirely different appearance when seen near to hand. As a low growing shrub, *Haastia* shows few of the characteristics of a normal plant of this type. The branches are all of the same height, growing so closely together that it is almost impossible to force a pencil point between the twigs. Thick overlapping woolly leaves hide the branches. Exposed surfaces are covered with long wool-like hairs protecting the plant against extreme cold. Rooted to the underlying rock, it covers an area anywhere from 2 to 8 square metres. *Haastia* is virtually immune to wind damage no matter what icy blizzards may blow across its normal habitat. It is a native of the subalpine and alpine fellfields of the mountains of Nelson and Marlborough and found nowhere else. *Haastia* is named after Sir Julius Haast, geologist to the Provincial Government of Canterbury. A great number of other prostrate growing plants are to be found in the country, many in environments not particularly suited to the adaptations that have evolved. This, once again, demonstrates the rapidity of past climatic changes and the time lag that takes place in the adaptation of plants to suit new conditions.

Spiked, hooked and spiny plants:

Spikes, spines, hooks and prickles are generally regarded as adaptations of a plant to protect itself from the depredations of animals. Yet it is fairly certain that for the last several million years New Zealand has been free of all mammals and other animal herbivores likely to damage plant life. Despite this a number of native plants have an impressive armoury of offensive weapons.

TARAMEA (*Aciphylla* spp.): The Wild Spaniard or Speargrass. A genus found throughout New Zealand, most characterised by fearsome tufts of sword-like leaves of up to half a metre in length. The ring of sharp lances which these plants present are an almost perfect defence against animals in the adult plant, but in the juvenile stage the leaves are flaccid and grass-like and eagerly eaten by sheep and cattle. It is thought that with the absence earlier of grazing animals in New Zealand, the spikes are an adaptation to arid conditions. Xerophytic plants as adapted to arduous drought conditions are fairly common in this country and this, combined with geological evidence, points to much of the eastern South Island having been a desert in some remote past.

TŪMATAKURU (*Discaria toumatou*): The Wild Irishman is as equally a fearsome shrub as The Wild Spaniard. It is a much branched, rigid shrub carrying sharp thorns that are so hardy that the early Māori used them as tattooing needles. The branches are tangled and interlaced and leaves are sparse excepting in Spring. A young plant growing in a damp atmosphere does not develop spines and this clearly points to a Xerophytic adaptation at some past time.
It can attain a height of three metres which probably explains its expressive Māori name "Tūmatakuru" or "Standing Face-Beater". Generations of Māori wore flax capes and leggings of cotton plant, flax or silver tussock to ward off the attentions of this adversary.

Mt. Cook Lily, Pōhutukawa Blossoms (National Archives)

Above: Ferns, the trail, and trampers on Milford Track.
Below: Kahikatea with flax in foreground (National Archives).

Above: Southern Rātā at Franz Josef, South Westland.
Below: Puawānanga flowers (both National Archives).

Tī Kōuka, Cabbage Tree (National Archives).

Kauri Tree, Omahuta Reserve, measuring 16 metres to first limb and 11 metres in girth, (National Archives).

TĀTARĀMOA (*Rubus cissoides* etc.): The Bush Lawyer. A New Zealand genus of the rose family. All varieties of bush lawyer are distinguished by being easier to get into their clutches than get out of them. The practical reason is that all are liberally provided with twining stems and backward curved prickles. The various species grow in and around heavy forest, the hooks being so shaped as to allow the lianes to readily slip upwards on a support but inhibit a downward movement. By this means does a plant climb over bushes, trees and itself, forming a nearly impenetrable mass. This is yet another series of plants showing gross adaptation to environment.

Tātarāmoa, when it grows in heavy forest, extends out a leafy trailing liane reaching considerable heights through climbing nearby trees. If grown in open country it changes to a mound of interlacing stems with leaves reduced to midribs covered with yellow hooked prickles. A further peculiarity is that it flowers only under the cover of the forest canopy and never in the open. See flower photo page 31.

The Māori name of "tātarāmoa" is applied also to the introduced gorse and blackberry. It is referred to in the karakia recited about the separation of the Sky Father (Rangi) and the Earth Mother (Papa) where Papa is advised to "shrink from her lover Rangi as the skin does from the nettle and the bramble". Māori lore also intimates that the first covering of the Earth that Papa inherited was just prickles of one description or another.

Parasites and Epiphytes:

These are a group of plants that exist not on the food they produce themselves but on the nourishment produced by other plants. Since parasites do not require the normal food-producing leaves of other plants they are often inconspicuous, consisting of little more than specialized roots which enter the woody tissue of the host plant and those flower structures suited to their method of reproduction. New Zealand is richly endowed with parasitical plants in comparison to most temperate countries and a few of them are described on the following pages.

KORUKORU (*Elytranthe colensoi*): The Scarlet Mistletoe, to give it its common English name, is a member of the family Loranthaceae from whence comes the mistletoe of the Druids they believed to be sacred and born in the spirit world. Scarlet Mistletoe is found mainly in New Zealand's beech forests and produces beautiful and brilliant flowers in considerable abundance. These forests are remnants of the Antarctic influence on native vegetation and are much more open, yet gloomier, and altogether different from other forests in the country. *Elytranthe colensoi* is parasitic on *Pittosporum* trees in the North Island and *Northofagus* in the South Island.

The Scarlet Mistletoe forms large bushes in the top of these trees and the blossoms are so profuse and so abundant as to hide the foliage, a jewel-like mass of glowing scarlet blossoms dotted among the sombre green of the forest canopy. The Māori name "Korukoru" refers to the mistletoe when in flower. In the South Island the name is "Pikirangi", short for "Piki ki te rangi" - "climb to the sky". It is said that the plant was the last left in Tāne's basket when he sowed the forests. He looked at it tenderly and said: "I cannot let my last child lie on the ground", and that is why it is a parasitic plant that perches high on the big trees.

PIRITA (*Ileostylus micranthus*): Unlike the Scarlet Mistletoe, this Small-Flowered Mistletoe produces minute green flowers. It is remarkable mainly for its method of germination. The ripe seed is contained in a yellow sticky fruit eagerly sought by birds. The seeds pass through the digestive tract of the bird and are deposited with their droppings on branches of nearby trees. The seed rest dormant beneath a varnish coating which affixes it to the branch until the process of germination has exhausted the food in the seed. At this time thin tendrils creep from the seed along the branch of the host tree and even down the main trunk. At intervals the suckers penetrate the tissue of the host and woolly lumps are formed covered by scales. Where the branches of the parasite touch, they join, so forming a complex network of stems. This plant can be called semi-parasitical as it produces masses of glossy green flowers.

RĀTĀ (*Metrosideros robusta*): The Northern Rātā usually starts out life as an epiphyte, its tiny seed resting in a hollow high in the branches of another tree. In time it becomes a tall tree itself, often, but not always, crushing the host tree. In the same family, but not an epiphyte, is the famed crimson-flowered pōhutukawa, see photo page 19. However, the adaptive ability of *Metrosideros robusta* makes this particular plant of special importance.

The seeds are so small that they are readily blown before the wind. Should a seed land in suitable ground, free from too much competition, it will germinate and eventually develop into a strong growing, crooked-looking but moderate sized tree, bearing masses of brilliant scarlet flowers. Should the seed fall into the fork of a suitable tree, high in the air, it will, if conditions are right, germinate there among the moist rotten leaf remains that collect in such places. As the plant develops, it drops roots towards the ground often 20m. or more below. As the roots reach ground level and begin to nourish the plant, further roots are dropped until the host tree is completely surrounded by the root system of the rātā.

Because the host tree was mature at the time of the germination of the rātā and subject to competition for light, it is very often dies ahead of its competitor, owing to the vigorous growing younger plant over-tapping the leaf system of the host. The rātā then stands as a free-growing tree in its own right, but often with a hollow trunk. No other plant, certainly no other tree, is known to have the dual capacity of either growing to a self-supporting tree in open country, or to begin as an epiphyte in the forest.

After a long life it is perhaps ironical that the rātā itself is often destroyed by the weight of mosses, perching lilies, ferns and other epiphytes that have fastened themselves to it – for it has roots just under the ground. There is a Māori saying about this fact, used to deride a person of little merit: "Well done shallow root" – you have no hold on the ground on which you stand - just like the rātā. Occasionally the bones of the Māori dead were buried among tree epiphytes, there being the belief that it was wrong to bury the dead in the ground, because the earth produces food for mankind.

KŌWHARAWHARA (*Astelia solandri*): This Perching Lily is an epiphyte not confined to New Zealand, but is here considered by many the most beautiful of all the *Astelia* family. It forms huge clumps of sword-shaped leaves 1-2m. long high up on the limbs and trunks of forest trees. The mass of leaves can be 2m. in circumference with the thick curved base of the leaf being ideal for water storage. Huge panicles of cream, sweetly scented flowers yield to a mass of intermingled red, yellow, and green berries much relished by the Māori. Their leaves were used in personal adornment as was the gum from the base of the leaves. The soft down from the same base was used for wrapping around a fractured limb.

Among other New Zealand epiphytes are a number of members of the Orchidaceae family. The two most appealing orchids are the Tree Orchid, *Dendrobium cunninghamii*, and Hanging Tree Orchid, *Earina mucronata*. The former produces many-flowered racemes of pale rose and white. The latter orchid has sweet scented flowers, cream in colour and a deeper cream, three-loped lip with an orange spot at the base. Both grow throughout the country in lowland forests.

The Ferns:

The lush tropical beauty of the New Zealand forest is characterised by the profusion of ferns growing in an almost infinity of form. It is strange to realise, after a trek through a New Zealand rain forest, that out of some 10,000 varieties of ferns found throughout the world, New Zealand has less than 200 different species, for in our forests ferns display an abundance of growth whereever one looks.

Ferns are of considerable antiquity, their ancestry descending relatively unchanged from the steamy swamp forest of Palaeozic times some five hundred million years in our past. It is important in tracing the pre-history of New Zealand to realise that the ferns of the country do trace an unbroken lineage back into those earliest times. There are a number of varieties of ferns found that are not known elsewhere and in other cases distribution is shared with other countries, a key to possible land bridges in the distant past.

While New Zealand's ferns may be classified as including creeping, climbing, perching and tufted varieties, it is the tree ferns that stand out, especially the two described here:

MAMAKU (*Cyathea medullaris*): The Black Tree Fern. The most magnificent and stately of our tree ferns. It has a slender trunk rising 20m. or more into the air and has a frond crown up to 14m. across. The mature trunk becomes a hard mass of tissue that gives great resilience to the fern. The soft part of the head of the trunk was at one time baked in the Māori hangi oven in blocks of about the length of a man's arm. Cooking time was up to twelve hours and the taste has been described as like dried apple with the texture of sago. Because the fern dies when its half-mature trunk is lopped off, the Māori protected the plant by imposing tapu restrictions to discourage indiscriminate harvesting.

PONGA (*Cyathea dealbata*): The Silver Tree Fern. Of lesser height than the Mamaku, the Ponga will nevertheless often top 10m. in height with fronds 2 to 4m. long. The fronds are silvery-white underneath and were once laid on the floors of Māori houses with the underneaths touching the floor so that spores would not blow around when the seed capsules burst.
Legend has it that both Ponga and Mamaku were once denizens of the sea but were forced to flee to the forests when pursued by Tāwhaki, the man-god with a lightning-like body. They apparently originally had upright standing fronds but were forced by the hakuturi, the forest elves, to assume a drooping position for some offence given.

The Rare and the Beautiful:

It is said with some truth that you have to look hard to find brilliant colours in our countryside. Various shades of green, flashes of red from rātā and pōhutukawa, and the bright yellow of the imported gorse bush predominate. However, hidden away are some beautiful flowers to be found – see over.

MT. COOK LILY (*Ranunculus lyalli*): See photo page 19. This is not a lily but a giant buttercup, a stately plant found throughout most of the South Island and Stewart Island. It is the largest ranunculus in the world and is extremely difficult to grow away from its normal habitat. Its waxy-white flowers measure 4 to 5cm. across, with twenty to sixty petals around short golden stamens. The leaves on the mature plant are saucer-shaped and 13 to 20cm. across.

MOUNTAIN DAISIES (*Celmisia* spp.): See photo page 31. A genus of aster-like plants producing single flower heads on each stem. There are about sixty species in New Zealand found mainly in the sub-alpine regions. In many of the species the flowers are large, white, many-petalled and very beautiful.

NATIVE CLEMATIS (*Clematis* spp.): New Zealand has nine native species of clematis, two of them bearing white flowers, all the rest have greenish-yellow or yellowish flowers. In none of these climbers are the flowers brightly coloured. The native varieties of this genus exhibit another peculiarity of New Zealand flora, the number of unisexual plants which are present. Flowers which contain stamens alone, or pistils alone, are far more common than in other lands and genera which are bisexual elsewhere are commonly unisexual in New Zealand. This is the case with the genus Clematis.

PUAWĀNANGA (*Clematis paniculata*): See photo page 21. This large white clematis is a spectacular sight when in flower and draped across the dull green of the trees that support it. The flowers rise in huge sprays with the male flowers up to 10cm. across, and the female slightly smaller. The seeds are carried in feathery wreaths of long silvery plumes nearly as beautiful as the flowers. The Māori called it "puawānanga", or "flower of legendary lore". "Wānanga" is a code of ethics dating back thousands of years. The plant is known as child of two stars in the heavens: Rehua, the father, a star whose appearance heralds summer; and Puanga, the mother, a star foretelling the kind of season in prospect, she is the food bringer.

HOUHERE (*Hoheria populnea* and related spp.): The Lacebark, a graceful tree growing up to 10m. in height, is named for the texture of its bark fibre. This is multi-layered and paper-like, and perforated with a series of holes akin to lace. The tree bears enormous quantities of flower clusters, white and deliciously scented. Māori took the lacey layers of inner bark, laid the strips cross-wise, and used the plant's natural glutinous sap to hold the strips together. Used in various ways in the lining of waist garments (piupiu) and capes (kākahu), to make headbands (tīpare) and poi balls (as a substitite for raupō), and for all sorts of bandages and slings. The toughness of its fibres and its reasonable resistance to damp led to it being plaited into ropes, nets, eel baskets etc. Its toughness was also a help on washday. A cape needing cleansing was steeped in water, uku, a blueish clay used as a soap was applied, and strips of lacebark used to beat the garment,

KOPAKOPA (*Myosotidium hortensia*): The Chatham Island Lily Forget-me-not is that rarity among the New Zealand flora, it has blue flowers. The whole plant has a striking appearance with its large, glossy kidney-shaped leaves standing almost 1m. above the root-stock. The flowers form large clusters 10 to 15cm. across. Each flower has a bright blue centre, fading to a lighter blue at the margin. The flower stalk carries the flower head some 60cm. high.

KŌWHAI-NGUTUKĀKĀ (*Clianthus puniceus*): Kākā Beak or Red Kōwhai is one of the most colourful of New Zealand's plants with its vivid red to pink flowers. The plant is of the pea family and is usually found as a rambling shrub, but sometimes has tree-like form. It has glossy fern-like leaves, with flower stalks hanging below the leaves bearing six to fifteen blooms. Each flower is boat-shaped, about 7cm. long, and full of nectar to attract the honey-eating birds that pollinate the plants. Banks and Solander, the scientist and botanist on Captain Cook's first voyage of exploration to New Zealand collected Kākā Beak in 1769. It is now almost extinct in the wild, but thrives in home gardens for its showy flower display.

KŌWHAI (*Sophora microphylla, S. tetraptera, S. prostrata* etc.): See photo on opposite page. Yellow Kōwhai is our national flower and like the Red Kōwhai is a member of the pea family, with which it also shares roughly the same shape flower parts. It varies in height from 2 to 12m. and has a seasonally variable flowering pattern depending on the species concerned and its location.

Kōwhai flowers appear before its leaves and as the tree enjoys a solitary habitat standing alone on river banks and near the edge of forests, it makes a striking picture in full bloom. The Māori in their poetry and proverbs call this display "kōwhai rains" and its first appearance "the kindling of the kōwhai fires". Birds fertilise this tree, attracted by the copious supply of nectar within the flowers.

MĀNUKA (*Leptospermum scoparium*) and **KĀNUKA** (*Kunzea ericoides*): Red Mānuka and White Mānuka (Kānuka) are both members of the myrtle family and both colloquially are called "Teatree" because early explorers and settlers brewed a spicy tea from their leaves. Both grow as shrubs or trees, Red Mānuka being the smaller of the two, but having larger single flowers of white or pink colour and no scent. Kānuka bears its white or pale cream flowers more densely in clusters and is sweet smelling.

Both mānuka and kānuka are children of Tāne, lord of the forest, and Hurimaiteata, according to much Māori lore. The uses of the plants were myriad. The wood was used for splints, fishing rods, paddles, pallisade palings, weapons of war etc. A popular firewood, as it burns easily, its ash may be rubbed on the scalp for skin diseases. The leaves and twigs are infused for an effective diuretic.

Above left: Kōwhai in flower, Crown Copyright: Department of Conservation, Te Papa Atawhai 2004.
Above right: Tātarāmoa, Bush Lawyer Flowers, Lake Sumner Forest Park (National Archives)
Below left: Mountain Daisies (National Archives)
Below right: Bush Orchid (National Archives)

Fauna

Fauna is the collective name for animals of a region; to most people animals means lions and tigers, cats and dogs, antelopes and rhinoceros. It is possible to say, in popular terms, that like snakes in Ireland, animals in pre-historic New Zealand were non-existent. However, living creatures generally recognized as animals are (in scientific terms) but one class of the kingdom of living things. The other kingdom is the plant kingdom and from this it follows that fauna makes reference to every living thing not classified as a plant. So a biologist would not say that "before the coming of man there were no animals in New Zealand" but, "there is no evidence to show that in primitive New Zealand there ever existed any indigenous mammals".

The scientific group called "Mammalia" is but one division of the animal kingdom. The class mammalia is that group of animals having milk-secreting organs for the suckling of their young. Mammals are the highest class of animals and include all the larger animals with the exception of a few fish. In this sense it is reasonable to state that New Zealand possesses no native mammals. Even this statement is open to doubt for there are two endemic species of bats found in the country, but as bats can fly and at least one species is to be found in Eastern Australia as well, it is possible that neither of the species of bats are true natives.

The absence of any members of the class mammalia, is curious, to say the least, and has had a powerful influence on the adaptations of other animals that are true natives to the once isolated islands that make up New Zealand. Still speaking in general scientific terms, one can speculate that "the ecological gap left by the absence of mammals has been partly filled by the class Aves (the birds)". Ecology is that branch of biology dealing with relations between living things and their environment. It includes both animals and plants. The biological class "Aves" refers only to that class of animal in which most members possess structural specialization for flight and the skin is clothed with feathers.

In filling an ecological niche (which in other countries is taken up by mammals), New Zealand native birds have adapted in ways which have resulted in many species being unique in comparison to other members of their class throughout the world.

The dependence of other living species on bird life is greater in New Zealand than in any other observed area. One authority describes sixty-five percent of native trees as depending on birds for seed dispersal. In other words, the propagation of well over half of the native forest trees requires that the avifauna eat the fruit of the plant, pass the seeds through the digestive system and deposit the seeds in the droppings at some distance from the parent tree.

Honey eating birds are important in effecting pollination of a large number of native plants as discussed in the last section on flora and many birds are specially adapted to feed off certain types of forest and tree inhabiting insects. In addition the particular ecology of New Zealand has given rise to a number of species in which the power of flight has been lost. Many different factors created in the past have produced varieties of native birds of considerable interest to both amateur and professional ornithologists and a number of examples of these interesting birds are discussed shortly.

New Zealand Birds:

Probably arising from the country's geographical isolation over so long a period, and in part owing to the general uniformity of the primitive forest cover of most of the land, there is a comparative paucity of native bird species. There are less than 250 species of birds regarded as native, and over half this number are sea birds, who perhaps should not be classed as truly endemic.

Even when uniquely indigenous to New Zealand, a comparatively high proportion of the avifauna are sub-species of Australian species. In this southern temperate region of the world, the weather system causes a consistent migratory animal pattern from west to east and at times the activity of this easterly movement is high. Since the time of European occupation, it is known that at least a dozen Australian species have been blown across the Tasman Sea to New Zealand. As most of these recent arrivals have settled and bred successfully here, one can theorise that the same process of colonisation has continued since early geological times. One must also take into account the existence of the land bridge that linked this country with others, the super-continent Gondwanaland.

Some indication of the length of time that a particular species has been isolated can be obtained by studies of the differences between the endemic species and related species elsewhere. Such evidence, along with the findings of palcantologists and their studies of fossilized remains, have established the very great antiquity of a few native bird species. Among such species of birds that continue to survive, the kiwi has the distinction of being the oldest inhabitant of the country still extant, with the possible exception of the tuatara, a native reptile, of which more will be said later.

KIWI (Family Apterygidae):
At present the following species and subspecies are recognised:

NORTH ISLAND BROWN KIWI (*Apteryx australis mantelli*)
Common name: Kiwi
SOUTH ISLAND BROWN KIWI (*A. australis australis*)
Common names: Kiwi, Tokoeka
STEWART ISLAND BROWN KIWI (*A. australis lawryi*)
Common name: Tokoeka. Only kiwi to come out regularly at daytime.
LITTLE SPOTTED KIWI (*A. owenii*)
Common name: Kiwi-pukupuku. Smallest kiwi.
GREAT SPOTTED KIWI (*A. haastii*)
Common name: Roa. Largest kiwi. See photo on page 3.

The kiwi species is the only living member of the order Apterygiformes. It started to evolve some seventy to eighty million years ago and from fossil remains it appears likely that the kiwi has existed little changed in appearance from that time. The tragedy is that all species of kiwi are dropping rapidly in numbers in the wild and do not seem likely to be around for another eighty million years, if decimation from mankind's activities and animal pests continues. All species have many similarities but also great differences. Alike, the mature bird stands less than half a metre high; has a rather shaggy appearance owing to its hair-like feathers which lack the barbules that hold the feathers together in most birds; possesses no tail; and has evolved for so long in a flightless pattern that the wings are quite useless and hardly visible.

A curious characteristic are the nostrils, being placed at the tip of a long flexible beak. In most birds nostrils are situated high up near the base of the beak. The low positioning of the opening in the case of the kiwi offers considerable advantages in the search for its staple food – worms or grubs. In addition the tip of the beak is sensitive to touch and this is of further assistance in feeling for its victim. This beak adaptation is associated with the kiwi's nocturnal habits and its very poor eyesight.

The legs of the bird are powerful and clumsy-looking and quite unsuited for flight, but effective in defence when scrapping with another kiwi for territory. They have can run very fast and kick with tremendous force, and have been known to split a man's hand open. Nevertheless, the kiwi does not have adequate defences against the attacks of pigs, dogs, feral cats, ferrets and opossums.

The egg of the kiwi is six times the size of a hen's egg and weighs around one quarter of its body weight. It is the largest egg in proportion to the size of a bird that is known, and takes between 75 and 80 days to hatch. The female leaves the nest after laying her egg (usually two in the case of the North Island Brown Kiwi) and the male takes over the job of hatching the egg(s). A chick born cannot hold its weight on its legs until four days old and is not fed by its parents. It can however search for worms itself from the 6th day.

The kiwi, although it had no natural enemies until the Polynesians introduced dogs and rats, is well camouflaged with its dark grey to brown feathers. Both the North and South Island kiwi have similar bird calls: the male a short, shrill whistle "kiwi, kiwi" heard at dusk for a couple of hours to advertise and confirm his territory, calls repeated four or five times, then he goes silent until morning. The female utters much the same tune but in a lower and hoarser tone. The Little Spotted Kiwi has a quite different voice: the male a high-pitched call that rises in musical scale at its end, each call a second or two in duration; the female a little lower in tone and more tremulous.

The normal habitat of the kiwi is in deep forest and around forest edges. The nests are made in natural hollows, under logs, stones, tree roots and banks, and if no suitable site for nesting is to be found, the birds will work in pairs to excavate a burrow in soft ground. In sleep the bird lies with its feet bent under the body and the head directed backwards; the bill is pressed close to the side, and lies above the wing, and not beneath it, whereas in certain flightless birds, like the penguin, the bill lies below the wing.

The Māori call the kiwi "the hidden bird of Tāne (the forest god)" - *Te manu huna a Tāne* - for after being conceived of the union of Tāne and Haere Awa Awa, it made its home in the darkest recesses of the forest. With its perfect camouflage it can certainly remain there unseen by human eyes. For this reason the saying is quoted to describe a person who has arrived somewhere unnoticed.

The kiwi is known today as a bird having a cone-shaped head, long bill, rudimentary wings and no tail. Māori folk lore tells us that once the kiwi was large and beautiful, with strong wings and flowing tail feathers. A vain bird, it would spend much of its time beside a clear water pool admiring itself. One day the kiwi was asked to go on an errand by the chief of the fairy people of the forest. He was required to ask all the fairy clans to gather for a meeting. He refused and as penalty for his bad behaviour the chief caused kiwi's wings and tail feathers to drop off, and his body feathers to became dull and lifeless. A cautionary tale indeed!

MOA (Dinornithiformes): It may be argued that an extinct bird should not be included in a discussion on the avifauna of a country, but there are at least three good reasons why this should be done. Firstly, the moa is well known and often quoted by the authors of books on birds as representing one of the largest bird that is ever known to have lived. Secondly, moa remains are common in many parts of New Zealand and are on display in many museums. Lastly, the survival of this primitive land bird into comparatively recent times is a key to a goodly part of the ancient history of the land.

The moa, of which there were about eleven species, belong to two families, the Dinornithidae and the Emeidae. Its relation here is the kiwi (both in ratite family) and elsewhere the rhea of South America, the emu and cassowary of Australia and the ostrich of Africa. Further evidence of the existence of the super-continent Gondwanaland. The moa existed here in large numbers well into the time of the Māori, with remnant populations to be found up to some 500 years ago. Moa flesh was an important food for many centuries, but when the moa had been hunted to extinction, the Māori were forced to rely on protein foods of less potential. *Mate ā moa* or "lost like the moa" is an expression still used to describe hopeless, desperate loss.

Isolated for so long and with no competition from grazing animals, it is not surprising that a bird species would develop to take the place of the animals which roamed the plains of other countries. In many respects the largest of the moa, *Dinornis giganteus*, took the place of the bisons of the North American continent, the plains animals of Africa and the cattle of Europe and Asia.

Certainly *Dinornis giganteus* was a giant. Standing three metres high, it was taller than any present day animal excepting the elephant and the giraffe. It must have been an awe-inspiring sight. From the abundant remains of moa found in swamps and sink holes it appears that they lived on twigs, seeds, leaves and fruits taken from trees on the forest edges. Lacking teeth, they relied on up to 3kg. of gizzard stones to help masticate their food. With such an inefficient digestive system there can be no doubt that the giant moa must have had to work very hard indeed to stay alive and vunerable to new competitors.

TAKAHĒ (*Porphyrio mantelli*): (Page 41). The story of the takahē is that of the dead living again for it had been regarded as extinct for the best part of a century when re-discovered in November 1948.

A brilliantly hued bird with blue, blue-green and white plumage, a massive red bill and short strong red legs, the takahē is a large flightless bird rather larger than a rooster. The adult bird stands about 50cm. high and can weigh as much as 3kg. It was originally widespread throughout the country but by the time of European colonisation in the nineteenth century it was already a rare bird. Only four specimens had ever been taken by Europeans before 1948 and no further birds had been seen since the nineteenth century.

So the matter rested until an amateur ornithologist, Geoffrey Orbell, took an interest after hearing rumours of a strange-looking bird in the mountain fastnesses of Fiordland. He found the takahē in 1948 in the Murchison, Kepler and Stuart Mountains west of Lake Te Anau and was able to capture a pair of the birds. The population of takahē at that time was estimated to be around 250 to 300 birds. Their numbers declined rapidly so that by 1982 there were estimated to be only 112 birds, and their habitat had become confined to the Murchison Mountains. Since then the birds have been bred in captivity and small colonies of them translocated to island refuges off the North and South Islands. After deer control (who compete for the takahē's food, tussock grass), the current number in the wild is estimated to be still only 150 birds. Small numbers of takahē may be seen in captivity at the Wildlife Centre in Te Anau, and at the National Wildlife Centre, Mt. Bruce, Masterton.

The birds usually mate for life, inhabit a restricted area, and are fiercely territorial. In summer they feed on alpine grasses, such as broad-leaved snow tussock, and in winter descend to the forest for shelter and to seek fern root. Takahē make their nests among snow tussock where each nesting pair builds a raised nest. They do not begin breeding until their second year and the clutch will contain between one to three eggs, eighty per cent of which will hatch. Only one chick is likely to survive the first winter. The bird can live for twenty years, but few do in the wild.

PŪKEKO (*Porphyrio porphyrio*): See photo page 42. Although classified by ornithologists as in a different family to the takahē, the pūkeko bears close resemblance to that bird, but in contrast to it the pukeko has learnt to live in the presence of man, and, being lighter and more agile, is easier able to fend off other animal predators.

The physical similarities are in plumage, bone structure, muscle development and the like. As well, both the takahē and the pūkeko are infested by fairly rare types of feather lice and certain internal parasites are shared by both birds. Then again, their habit of eating is unusual but shared, in that plant food is held in one claw and bitten off. The habit is common among parrots but both the pūkeko and the takahē belong to the Rail family. Both are fast runners and good swimmers and make a characteristic flicking movement of the tail when disturbed.

The pūkeko is a swamp dweller and therefore very often known as the Swamp Hen. It is a laboured, clumsy flier, noisy, aggressive and vicious when it meets or is disturbed by smaller bird life. The plumage is an indigo blue and black. It has orange-red legs and feet, its bill is scarlet. It has a characteristic strut when walking, it swims with its tail high, and it feeds on water plants as a staple diet, but is not hesitant in attacking field crops.

In keeping with their general buccaneering character, the pūkeko builds a large untidy nest on a tussock or rush clump. Two or three hens sometimes share a nest and male and females mate freely within their group. Both sexes divide the labour during the incubating period and the feeding of the young, as many as sixteen chicks being raised by the community of mothers at one sitting.

Māori lore tells us that the pūkeko got its scarlet nose when Tāwhaki, an illustrious ancestor who seems to be much associated with the colour red, was on his way up to the lands of the twelve heavens. He met Pūkeko and his parents coming down and Pūkeko, ignoring the mana of great Tāwhaki, brushed against him. In retaliation Tāwhaki squeezed pūkeko's nose and that is why it has been a scarlet red colour ever since. The Māori caught the pūkeko by laying hair nooses attached to stakes over water areas frequented by the birds.

KEA (*Nestor notabilis*): See photo page 60. According to some Māori authorities, the kea was one of the birds that was captured by Tāne Matua, Tāne the Parent, after his fight with the Whānau Puhi, the "Wind Children" in the heavens, and thereafter brought to earth. One has to question whether this was a good choice for the kea is a known thief, a mischievous troublemaker, a vandal, and in all probability a murderer, but above all else he is a humorist, whether consciously or unconsciously. Indeed, to all except a bereaved farmer, grieving for the loss of his sheep to the suspect kea, this New Zealand mountain parrot is irresistibly good fun. For sheer swashbuckling the kea would be hard to beat, for a brave, strutting, noisy intelligent fellow he certainly is.

It is common for people to impute human motives to the actions of animals and such beliefs are called "anthropomorphic" and are quite rightly held to be suspect. However, it is difficult not to believe that much of the behaviour of kea is the result of sheer good humour and an expression of its joy of living. In "kea country" which includes the high uplands of the Southern Alps, the traveller has to be extremely wary of the treatment a band of these birds will give his unguarded belongings. Boots provide a favourite form of sport, with the laces pulled out, the eyelets carefully removed, and the uppers cut to pieces. A tent will provide endless hours of fun. A flock of kea will always investigate a strange object and a pitched tent attracts them immediately. One or more of them will attempt to alight on the sloping side and, failing to get a foothold, will slide down the slope, at first in some surprise, and then in delight, shrieking "Keee-aa, Ke-aa" as it does. Within moments the whole flock will join in, interspersing the fun with wild games of 'follow the leader'. If one bird's powerful talons catch in the canvas and tear it, the sound of ripping apparently intrigues the mob and soon all the birds are busy tearing the tent to pieces, among sounds of great glee.

The intelligence of the birds is phenomenal and gives us the opportunity to quote the best bird story ever. It is worth retelling for it is claimed to be true and certainly is quite within the ability of the birds to carry out. The story runs in this way: -

Top left: Bellbirds, Little Barrier Island;
Top right: Takahē, Peter Morrison Photo;
Centre: Gannets at Cape Kidnappers, Hawke Bay. Deborah Shuker Photo;
Left: Tūī at feeding trough, Little Barrier Island.
Top left, Top right & Left photos Crown Copyright: Dept. of Conservation, Te Papa Atawhai 2004.

Above: Morepork at nest cavity, Hen Island, Dick Veitch Photo, Crown Copyright: Department of Conservation, Te Papa Atawhai.

Left: Kōtuku, White Heron; *Below left*: North Island Weka; both Crown Copyright: Department of Conservation, Te Papa Atawhai; *Right*: South Island Fantail, photographed by Dave Crouchley, Crown Copyright: Department of Conservation, Te Papa Atawhai 2004.

Far left: Pūkeko; *Above*: Kēruru, New Zealand Pigeons, both Crown Copyright: Department of Conservation, Te Papa Atawhai 2004.

Above: Kākāpō female "Hoki" about 14 weeks old, Maud Island, photo by G.C. Climo, Crown Copyright: Dept. of Conservation, Te Papa Atawhai 2004; *Below left*: Native Land Snail; *Below right*: Skink on Stephens Island; *Bottom*: Lake Orbell, named after Geoffrey Orbell, see Tuatara Page 38. Last two from Dept. of Conservation, Te Papa Atawhai 2004.

A party of mountaineers resting in a hut became annoyed with a lone kea repeatedly bouncing on the corrugated iron roof, presumably for the satisfying boom each bounce produced. Tiring of the noise, one of the men banged on the underside of the roof with the handle of a broom. Came silence and then at the top of the window, hanging upside down from the spouting, appeared the head and beady eyes of the kea. Nothing was to be seen of the cause of the noise and the kea returned to his former game. Again, the broom thumped, again the inquisitive eyes at the window; still nothing to be seen. This happened several times, the mountaineers taking pleasure in fooling the bird. At last the bouncing on the roof and the eyes at the window occurred together, the bird had got a companion to join him and carry on bouncing, while he investigated the cause of the echo.

The kea is a large bird, somewhat greater than 40cm. in length, the male being larger than the female. It possesses a long powerful beak, strong talons, is olive green in colour highlighted with scarlet undersides to the wings. The young have broader dark edgings to their feathers. Its calls are varied, highly unmusical, with the most plaintive call "keee-aa" predominating, clearly sounding as if it is the injured party. It nests in rock crevices at sub-alpine levels and has a clutch of 2 to 4 eggs. The fledgling period runs from 90 to 100 days. The life span of the bird is up to 20 years.

The bird's habitat was originally in alpine forest regions in the three main islands of New Zealand, but it is now to be found only in zones of South Island's mountain ranges. The Māori found the flesh of the kea a bit lean but did capture it in alpine solitudes by spreading a white garment on the ground, which, with its inquisitive nature, it investigated, and thus was captured.

Primarily it is a vegetarian but will eat flesh when chance allows, making it the only known carnivorous member of the parrot family. It is probable that its known liking for fat causes it to attack weakened or sick sheep for their kidneys, but although this suspicion has been held to be well-founded for a century and more, there is still much doubt as to how prevalent is the practice. It is likely that the taste for sheep's kidneys is confined to only a few kea, not all.

FANTAIL (*Rhipidura fuliginosa*): See photo page 43. Surely one of the most delightfully cheeky, irrepressible, restless birds of the world – one of its Māori names "tītakataka" means "flitting about" – the little fantail is a familiar friend of every New Zealander. *Rhipidura fuliginosa*, the South Island subspecies, is found in two colours, pied and black, the latter comprising 12 to 25 per cent of the population. *R. placabilis*, the North Island Fantail, is pied and is lighter brown on top than the South Island bird. Occasionally a completely white fantail is seen, these are considered by some Māori to be the spirit of a person who has recently died.

The natural habitat of the fantail is the bush edge and open clearings. It is not afraid of people and has prospered accordingly. Not being in any way shy, it will readily venture into a domestic garden, orchard or into the interior of a house. When flying, the fantail keeps its tail closed as it makes a series of aerial darts, dashes and acute changes in flight while in pursuit of insects. By far its most distinctive feature is the expansive tail which spreads out in a fan shape when the bird is manoeuvring in flight to change direction or to stop abruptly to take its insect prey.

The outstanding characteristic of the bird is the inquisitive, insolent attitude it displays. It hops and darts, dives in flight to pick up an insect, returns to the original spot, flits off erratically and all the time it keeps up a squeaky little *ti ti* chirp. Occasionally a fantail will adopt a house, if the family are away. He will make himself at home indoors and never enter into that bumbling panic-stricken flight which other species of birds display when trapped in a room. The only object that will disturb a fantail's aplomb is the sight of its own reflection in a mirror.

The fantail is a busybody and cannot help chirping away at all times. When folk hero Maui went to slay the goddess of death, Hinenuitepō, so that mankind might live forever, fantail accompanied him. Despite being asked to keep quiet beforehand, the fantail could not help chirping away as Maui was preparing to slay his sleeping opponent. So it was that Hinenuitepō awoke, Maui was killed, and mankind lost the opportunity of eternal life. That is the fantail for you!

KĀKĀPŌ (*Strigops habroptilus*): See photo page 44. The kākāpō – New Zealand's ground parrot – is yet another oddity. It is the only member of the Psittacidae family, is not related to other parrots, having this family name all to itself. It is the only flightless parrot in the world, the only nocturnal parrot, the only parrot where the male has inflatable thoracic sacs, the only parrot to practise "lek" mating, and the heaviest parrot in the world, weighing up to 3kg. Finally, it is a critically endangered bird, with all remaining kākāpō now living on outlying islands where the Department of Conservation does its best to keep them safe from predators.

The kākāpō is a large heavy-bodied bird with a dark green head, upper parts of the body are brown-green and its back and wings are light greenish-yellow. The feathers are mottled with brown and pale yellow bars. Its rather drab apparel should help it hide easily from predators, but it is often found because of its strong body smell. It has whiskers like a cat that assist it in its feeding and in going in and out of its holes, useful since it is a nocturnal feeder – kākāpō means "parrot of the night" - and it has a certain owl-like cast of feature that has given it the name "owl parrot". The shape of its brown facial disc helps the bird see at night. It does not fly but can climb a tree using its wings for balance so it does not fall.

Kākāpō are vegetarians. They are solitary birds, male and female living apart. They can mate only in years when the fruits of the rimu and kahikatea (white pine) are plentiful. Their courting takes place at a "lek" or arena courting bowl. The male selects a natural hollow to enlarge, which he does with his beak, then carefully removes all sticks and leaves to make the bowl as wide and smooth as possible. When this is ready the male inflates his chest like a balloon and makes a series of low-pitched booming sounds, at the same time as beating his wings on the ground. These displays to attract females take place from December to March in good fruiting years. The booming can last all night and continue for several months. The sound carries up to 5km. A female hearing the booming may come to visit, and if attracted to the male, will mate with him. A male may mate with several females during the booming season.

The female lays from 2 to 4 white eggs, and incubates the eggs for around thirty days. When the fledglings are two weeks old, she begins to make trips away from the nest in search of food, a time when the chicks are most vulnerable to enemies. Chicks may stay with the mother for as long as seven months. The kākāpō has a long life, it can reach 60 years.

Up to European times the Māori hunted the kākāpō with the small Polynesian dog. The booming sequences made the birds an easy target. In dry weather they were caught when they were having dust baths. Kākāpō were also taken by intercepting them as they traversed their well-defined trails to their nests from fern to stream and back. In those days the kākāpō lived together in flocks and kept a tīaka, or guardian sentry bird, when out feeding to warn them of approaching danger. He kept guard from the branch of a tree, dropping down to the feeding birds should danger threaten. The flesh of the bird was said to taste rather like lamb.

KĒRURU (*Hemiphaga novaeseelandiae*): See photo page 43. The New Zealand Pigeon is present in many parts of the country in small numbers. It has a striking appearance: the breast is white and the feathers of the head, neck, back and wings are iridescent, showing a range of colouring varying from gold, to copper, to green and purple. Heavy in flight, and clumsy in walking, its crashing through the foliage is easily detected. Its cry is a gentle "kuu", its young are hatched singly in a rough nest. A berry eater, the kererū is important for the dispersal of the seeds of native trees. Once the main food bird of the Māori it was captured simply by waiting until the birds had gorged themselves on ripe fruit when they could be easily snared or simply knocked off their perches. In winter and spring they were not taken as they had feasted on kōwhai leaves which imparted an unpleasant flavour to the flesh and gave the eater a headache! The birds have been given full protection since 1921.

Pigeon feathers were used by the Māori to adorn the cloaks called kahu kūkū and woven into many other garments. They adorned canoes, ceremonial houses, the tewhatewha, a weapon of war, etc.

RIFLEMAN (*Acanthisitta chloris*): New Zealand's smallest bird and a member of the wren family. It weighs just 6g. and is not much larger than a man's thumb. It is hardly ever seen but its high pitched call, most nearly rendered as "zipt-zipt-zipt-zipt", may be heard in the beech forests of the South Island. The head is yellow-green with a white streak over the eye, its back is green, its rump yellow. The bill is upturned and dark brown in colour. It flies feebly with a quivering motion of the wings.

TŪĪ (*Prosthemadera novaeseelandiae*): See photo page 41. In Māori mythology the tūī is a guardian of the door to the most sacred twelfth heaven. The bird has an extensive range of bell-like tones and a variety of calls; it is a great mimic. It was taught to speak by the Māori and memorised songs, proverbs, axioms, and genealogies. Its utterings were carefully heeded because of its godly connections. By colonists it was called the Parson Bird partly because of the clerical appearance given by the collar of white throat feathers, and also for its eloquent voice. Its plumage is metallic greenish-black, but it appears fully black at a distance. It is a restless, noisy, swift-moving and pugnacious bird. A honey eater, it has to travel long distances these days to find the nectars it prefers.

BELLBIRD (*Anthornis melanura*): (Page 41). The most beautiful songbird of the New Zealand bush, the bellbird has a range of liquid bell-like notes. A single bird's call is not outstanding but when large flocks of bellbirds utter their glorious concert of sound at sunrise or dusk in backblock New Zealand, one knows one is in the presence of a magic ecstasy of song. It is a honey eater, a smallish bird (about 20cm long), not striking in appearance with its olive-green coloration, and not easily distinguished among the foliage of the forest.

The bellbird was known as a spirit bird by the Māori, one able to carry messages to and from the gods. A famous proverb refers to this connection "the bellbird may be small but it can rise to the top of the kahikatea tree". In the practical sense, one knows the bellbird enjoys the small, sweet berries on the tips of its upper branches .

MOREPORK (*Ninox novaeseelandiae*): See photo page 42. Visitors staying in rural areas of New Zealand are often intrigued by the mournful, eerie call of this night-flying native bird. Its lonely desolate call (for all the world like a disembodied spirit calling for "more pork") can conjure up visions of a timeless primitive land in the imagination. Belonging to the order Strigiformes, or owls, the morepork has most of the characteristics of other owls.

The plumage is dull and its silent flight passage comes because of the downy feathers at the edge of the wings. Large eyes with golden irises reduce the pupils to pin-size during the daytime. Moreporks are carnivorous and the coming of large settlements has proved of benefit in increasing the supply of vermin and introduced small birds for food so that the species is increasing in number. They are seldom about by day. They can sometimes be seen under attack by other birds when caught away from the holes in trees in which they usually shelter during the daytime.

Like the kiwi, another night bird, the morepork is called "the hidden bird of Tāne" (lord of the forest). Two of its Māori names are "ruru", and "peho". Its first home was in the Underworld where Tāne and his brothers lived after separating their parents Rangi and Papa.

WEKA (*Gallirallus australis*): (Page 43). A flightless member of the rail family, and therefore related to the pūkeko and the takahē, the weka is now an endangered bird on the main islands of New Zealand.. It has become a casualty of the attacks of stoats and ferrets, cats and dogs. It shows little fear of man, a natural clown, mischievous, thieving and highly entertaining. It walks with an upright carriage, alternately raising and lowering the tail. Its colour varies according to species: the North Island is smallish and reddish-brown; the Western weka of the South Island has a chestnut phase and a black phase, is reddish-brown under. Its habitat is forest land, scrub and sand dunes and it likes a wide diet of insects, small animals, shellfish, fresh carrion and berries. Weka take delight in removing small objects from unwary campers and picnickers. One visitor lost bread, butter - and knife while watching a hawk flying overhead!

GANNET (*Morus serrator*): See photo page 41. This seabird breeds in New Zealand, Norfolk Island and Australia. The gannet reserve at Cape Kidnappers is the most accessible mainland colony of these birds in the world, drawing many visitors, but the birds also nest in some 20 gannetries around New Zealand. They are overall white in colour with a yellow head and black-edged wings. They are a sight to see, when resting in their hundreds at their colonies, or diving deep into the water for fish, splashing water a couple of metres in the air. The Māori used gannet feathers in the hair and for covering lashings on their canoes. Tākapu, the Māori name of the bird, is also a figurative expression for a chief – *Ko te tākapu tēnei nana ngā kōrero nui* – "It is the chief who does the talking".

KŌTUKU (*Egretta alba*): (Page 42). The White Heron breeds only at Okarito on the West Coast of the South Island, but is found in many countries. Because it is rarely seen, and is so beautiful, many Māori sayings are repeated about the kōtuku. "A kōtuku is seen but once" refers to an illustrious person who visits rarely. "Graceful as a kōtuku in flight" is a compliment to a person. "She stood on the brink of the water like a white heron" was a compliment paid Hinemoa as she stood at Lake Rotorua before swimming to her lover Tūtānekai.

New Zealand Bats:

The only mammals ever known to have been endemic to New Zealand are two species of native bats, a third is now extinct. Both living species are now rare and were taken by the Māori for food only in lean times. They called bats Pekapeka, associating them with the mythical hōkioi, a night-flying bird foretelling death and disaster.

LONG-TAILED BAT (*Chalinolobus tuberculatus*): (Page 56). Its name refers to the membrane running the whole length of its tail which is used to scoop up insects. The other surviving native bat has a short free tail. This bat weighs 8 to 11 grams. It can fly at 60km. per hour as it seeks out its food of midges, mosquitos and moths.

SHORT-TAILED BAT (*Mystacina tuberculata*): Larger than the long-tailed and weighing more, 12 to 15 grams. One of the few bats in the world to be able to climb and walk by folding the forepart of its wings and using them as legs. It seeks its diet of insects and fruit on the forest floor in this way. This bat is also a capable flier.

Reptiles:

There are no traces of snakes ever having lived in New Zealand and the native reptiles are represented by three species of Tuatara, 26 species of Skinks (photo page 44), and 17 species of Geckos.

TUATARA (*Sphenodon punctatus* and one subspecies, & *S. guntherii*): See photo page 55. The tuatara has the longest unbroken ancestry of any living animal. It is a soft-skinned reptile whose family tree runs back two hundred million years into the Triassic period and it has remained virtually unchanged since that time. References to it being a lizard are inaccurate, it is a reptile although it resembles a lizard. The tuatara is a direct representative of the primitive group from which all reptiles arose. The oldest ancestor of the tuatara predates the giant dinosaurs of the age of reptiles, like the 12m. long giant dinosaur *Tyannosaurus rex*.

The tuatara is the only living member of the order Rhynchocephalia, which means "beak-headed animals". The shape of the skull of the tuatara is more like that of a turtle than a modern lizard. There are no true teeth, the function of the teeth being carried out by sharp serrations of bone. These bone serrations are more primitive organs than the socketed teeth of most animals that developed later. The jaw, in general, resembles a mandible-like beak, although it is not obvious from the outside.

A fully grown adult will be up to 280mm. long, or up to 600mm. including tail. The legs are short and strong. The young are hatched from eggs which take some thirteen months to hatch. Between ten to fifteen eggs are laid in a trench or small burrow and covered with leaves. The rib cage has the same protective function as the abdominal plates in turtles. The common characteristics of the tuatara and the turtle are not coincidental for turtles are the next most ancient type of animal (after the tuatara) still living today.

The tuatara has an abnormally developed pineal gland with a well defined lens, pigmented retina and other structures as found in a normal eye – the tuatara's famed "third eye". It is not certain what function this eye still has. It does not appear above the surface of the skin but there appears to be some sensitivity when a spot of light is thrown on the area of the skin above the gland. The pineal gland in man and animal is sensitive to light and regulates sleep, reproduction, aging etc.

The habits of the tuatara are rather unusual. It shares the occupancy of its earth burrow, one tuatara per burrow, with a sea bird. A particular sea bird does not disturb the tuatara it lives with, but will drive away any other bird that tries to enter the burrow. Māori belief is that the tuatara originates from the domain of Tangaroa, the sea lord. Tuatara's diet includes the very bird species it co-habits with, their eggs, their chicks, lizards, and a wide variety of insects.

Tuatara have a long life, somewhere between 60 and 100 years. They move very slowly, being cold-blooded, their body activity being affected by the temperature. While timid by nature, they will bite furiously if handled.

Native Frogs:

Small groups of the four species of our native frogs are to be found in isolated places, in forests and on outlying islands. They differ from the common frog by the fact that the tadpoles develop on land, rather than in water. The genus Leiopelma (see Inside Front Cover and page 56) is a primitive one. In the N. Z. species there is a modified life history whereby there is no free swimming tadpole stage as with other frogs. The eggs are laid under stones or logs in damp places. Tadpoles develop inside the eggs hatching into baby frogs after about six weeks. The adults are quite tiny, growing to around 4cm. in length. They have no eardrums, nor do they croak, just a soft chirp.

FLAX SNAIL (*Placostylus* spp.): Grows as big as 115mm; is chocolate to reddish-brown in colour and is solidly built in a tall spiral. It looks far more like a seashell than the external skeleton of a land animal (see photo page 44). The eggs of the flax snail are thin shelled, somewhat akin to a small bird's egg. The Māori call it Pūpū-harakeke. However it does not eat flax (harakeke), rather it shelters there. It likes living close to the sea, it also likes a broadleaf forest habitat. This snail is a vegetarian, its habitat restricted to parts of Northland and off-shore islands. Some of these colonies are on the verge of extinction due to the ravages of pigs, rats and mice. Rat poisoning and translocation to islands have been tried with varying success. Flax and other native species have been planted to try and increase its habitat.

The genus Placostylus is found only outside New Zealand on Lord Howe Island, New Caledonia, Vanuatu, Solomon Islands and Fiji. This area of distribution largely coincides with the hypothetical "Melanesian Continent" which forms part of a possible pre-historical land bridge between New Zealand and Melanesia. Nevertheless, this genus is not represented in Australia.

KAURI SNAIL (*Powelliphanta* spp.): Pūpū-rangi, to give the Kauri Snail its Māori name, does not eat any part of the kauri tree but is found in parts of Northland where kauri grow. In any case the ground around kauri would be too dry for one of the snail's favourite foods, earthworms, to live in. The kauri snail has a tongue-like radula, somewhat like a cat's tongue, covered with thousands of tiny rasping teeth which draw in its soft bodied prey. The largest kauri snails can grow as big as a man's fist. They may be seen at the Trounson Kauri Park, one hour's drive of Dargaville, Northland, the Herekino Forest, and the Manginangina Scenic Reserve adjacent to the Puketi State Forest. *Powelliphanta* comprise some 38 species distributed throughout New Zealand in small colonies. All members of the genus are carnivorous, living on other snails, slugs, worms and small insects. In contrast to the Flax Snail, the *Powelliphanta* species is found in Tasmania and Victoria, Australia, but not in Melanesia.

Tuatara. Photograph by Deborah Shuker.

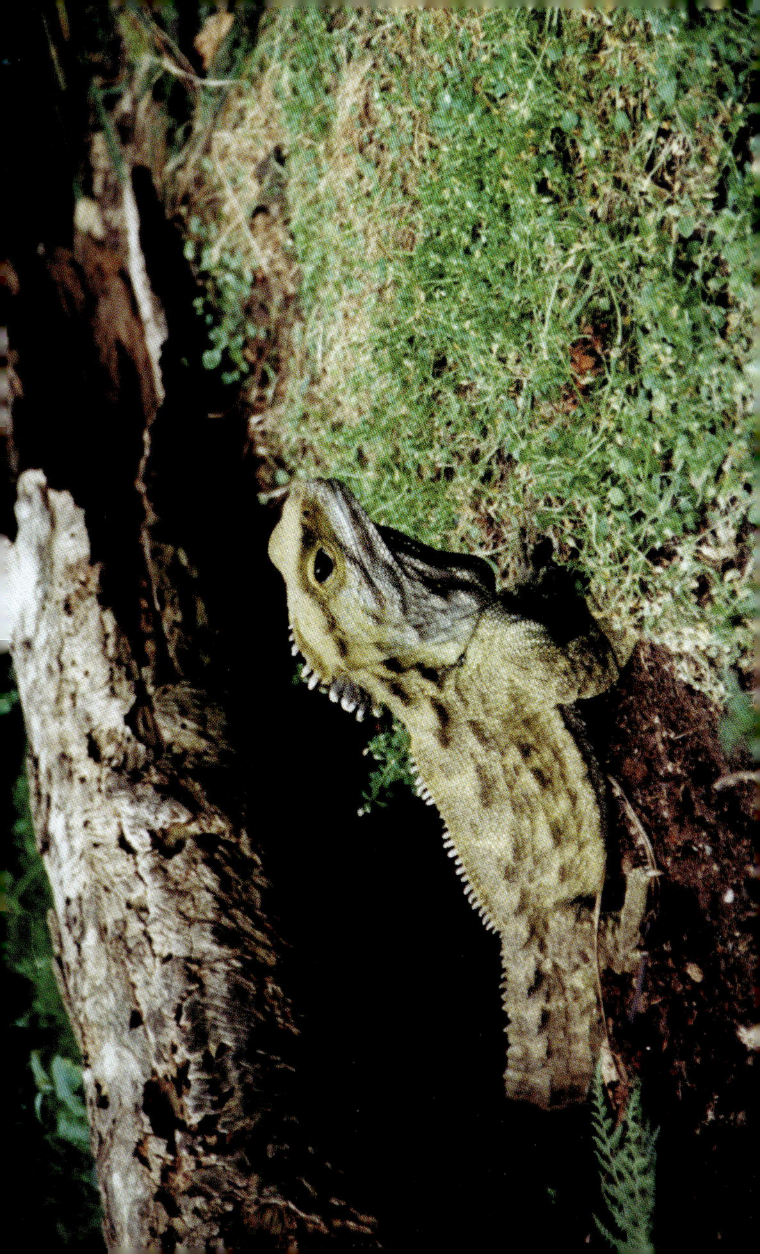

Above: Archey's Frog,
Leiopelma archeyi,
photo by D. Garrick;
Right: Giant Weta,
Little Barrier Island,
photo by J. C. Smuts-Kennedy;
Below: Long-Tailed Bat,
Chalinolobus tuberculatus,
photo by J. L. Kendrick.
All Crown Copyright:
Dept. of Conservation,
Te Papa Atawhai 2004.

New Zealand Insects:

The country has been generously supplied with insects, many of them completely unique. The distribution of related genera of insects, both inside and outside New Zealand, offers further evidence as to possible past connections between the lands of the Southern Hemisphere. Some 21,000 invertebrate species (mainly insects) have so far been described in New Zealand of a total estimated of 50,000 species that may exist. So many yet unknown who may disappear before measures can taken to save them. Some have however been identified for special attention. The Department of Conservation lists 26 species at risk including the flax and kauri snails just described, as well as various beetles, moths and weta.

ONYCHOPHORA A class of insects known as the Onychophora is considered to be the most primitive ancestral form from which all insects have evolved. In many respects the Onychophora stand in relation to other insects as the tuatara stands to other reptiles. These animals are generally small and lowly looking, something like a caterpillar or a worm with a row of stubby little legs down each side. Like worms, the Onychophorans move by extension and contraction of the body. They trap their prey by spitting out a viscid slime for up to 30cm. from glands on each side of their mouths. They then inject a toxic saliva into their prey which may be several times their size. Onychophora go back to the Cambrian period of time and specimens today differ little from originals found as fossils, with no intermediate forms. They are true "living fossils". The distribution of Onychophora is mainly in the Southern Hemisphere including equatorial West Africa, Mexico, central and northern parts of South America, the Melanesian Islands Groups, Tasmania, Australia and New Zealand, and perhaps odd man out, South East Asia.

Peripatus, or velvet worms, are a family of Onychophora found in Waikaia Forest, northern Southland. They live in the forest under moss or the bark of trees, or beneath or inside rotting logs. One of the most beautiful, *Ooperipatellus viridimimaculatus*, grows up to

75mm. in length. This species is found on the shores of Lake Te Anau and is resplendent with green spots on a velvet-like skin. It has 13 pairs of legs and is an egg-layer. *Peripatoides novaeseelandiae* has 15 pairs of legs, is velvety-looking in appearance and can reach 80mm. in length.

WĒTĀ Wētā is the informal name for two families of New Zealand grasshopper-like insects, one containing the Cave Wētā, the other the Giant, Tusked, Tree and Ground Wētā. These wētā, like the tuatara, pre-date the dinosaurs. They are among the heaviest insects in the world. In the past 150 years the extensive changes to land use have wiped out or endangered many insect species. A dozen of the Giant Wētā (*Deinacrida* spp.) and all three of the Tusked Wētā (*Hemiandrus* spp.) have become threatened because of the reduction of their forest and scrub habitats, by being trampled by stock, and eaten by rodents and stoats.

GIANT WĒTĀ (*Deinacrida heteracantha*): See photo page 56. The body of this insect, the size of a mouse, can be up to 100mm. in length with very long slender antennae, and weigh over 70 grams. On defence it stands almost straight up and gives an appearance which looks far more formidable than is actually the case.

TREE WĒTĀ (*Hemideina* spp.): Far more numerous than the giant wētā, the tree wētā is less than half the size of the former and lives in rotten logs and under the bark of trees. There are six species of tree wētā. It is the most likely species you can expect to find in your garden. The female has a long curved "tail", or rather ovipositor, for laying eggs, not for stinging its prey. The male has a very large head with a mandible, or lower jaw, it uses to bite and crush its food. It keeps a harem of up to ten females. The tree wētā makes a peculiar scraping sound by rubbing its hind legs against ridges on the sides of the body and this noise is quite characteristic of night noises heard in the New Zealand forest at certain times of the year. It is quite aggressive and will hiss and bite if disturbed. It is mostly vegetarian.

CAVE WĒTĀ (*Gymnoplectron edwardsii*): The cave, or jumping, wētā is an insect with an overall length of 50 to 65mm, much of which is made up of greatly elongated antennae and muscular hind legs. These are four times the length of the wētā's body. This wētā is a dweller of damp forest caves, damp bush or under stones in alpine regions. It is non-aggressive by nature and has remarkable jumping powers – it can jump up to two metres! It is a silent creature, has no ears, so cannot hear, and can live up to seven years. It is omnivorous in its eating habits; lichens and other organic matter are on its menu. While other wētā are normally noctural insects, the cave wētā will rummage around its home during the daytime.

GLOW-WORM (*Arachnocampa luminosa*): The Pūrātoke or Titiwai of the Māori. This glow-worm is unique to New Zealand and may be seen in many places by tourists. Two of the best-known displays are in the caves at Waitomo (near Te Kuiti) and Te Anau (in the Lake District of the South Island) where one is taken by boat to see the glow-worms. They require a specific habitat, a spot sufficiently damp for their survival, with hanging surfaces on which to lay eggs, and a through draught to bring insects to them. Glow-worms are the larvae of a two-winged insect of the fly family. They suspend themselves from the roofs of caves by sticky silken threads. The light comes internally and is projected through the transparent skin at the end of the abdomen to the threads for the purpose of luring minute insects. The gnat larvae pull in the thread on which the flying insect is caught when they sense vibrations of the thread. At the same time chemicals in the thread paralyse the victim. The light is caused by a chemical reaction involving several components. When glow-worms are very hungry their lights will shine more brightly. They also use their lights to dissuade other predators from eating them. At the end of about nine months the gnat larvae emerge from the pupa as flies about the size of a mosquito. These flies are also light-emitting and, after resting, they mate and the cycle starts all over again. Females attract males to mating using their lights. The flies have a lifespan of just two or three days.

HUHU BEETLE (*Prionoplus reticularis*): New Zealand's largest and heaviest beetle breeds in dead trees in native and exotic forests. It measures up to 50mm. in length at the adult stage. It sometimes comes inside houses, attracted by the light, and can give quite a nip with its conspicuous jaws if handled carelessly. The beetle burrows into dead wood, whether logs, stumps, or dead parts of living trees, to lay its eggs. The wood must have high moisture content. After hatching, the larvae chew their way through the rotten wood for two or three years to emerge as nocturnal beetles in Spring and Summer. The larvae are pale cream in colour and can reach a length of 50 to 75mm. They do a lot of damage to trees. Māori of the Tākitimu migration have the saying: "The kauri is long-lasting, the tōtara may harbour the huhu" (*Te kauri e haere wa, te tōtara e hāpai huhu*). Huhu grubs are a favourite delicacy of the Māori, raw or quick fried, and are said to taste like peanut butter. Bushmen of the West Coast of the South Island claim that huhu grubs have the best, most subtle, flavours when they come from the rimu and kahikatea trees that grow on the Coast. In old days the Maori used huhu grubs as a curative for a headache, frying them on a split stick over a fire. Mixed in the proportion of one-third pulp of hīnau berries and two-thirds huhu grubs a bread was made, and fed to invalids recovering from dysentery, diarrhoea or fever. The Maori also used the huhu grub as bait to catch eels, attaching the grub to a line of flax.

Below: Kea at McKinnon Pass, Milford Track, Fiordland, photo by John Edwards, Crown Copyright: Dept. of Conservation, Te Papa Atawhai 2004.